Animal Quintet

A southern memoir

COLIN DAYAN

COLIN

DAYAN

This is a LARB True Stories publication

Published by
The Los Angeles Review of Books
6671 Sunset Blvd., Suite 1521,
Los Angeles, CA 90028
www.larbbooks.org

ISBN 978-1940660721

Library of Congress Control Number:
2020935963

"Colin Dayan brings a rare combination to her work: a strong mind and an expansive heart."

—**Mark Edmundson,** University of Virginia. Author of *Why Read?* and *The Death of Sigmund Freud*

"Colin Dayan's *Animal Quintet* explores the complexity of race, class, gender, and region with relation to animality and history. What is it that we remember of pasts that have receded? What prompts such remembrance? How is the past always made present? Perhaps through feeling, through mood, through song. Focusing on animals and the relations they share with humans, the distinctions between are interrogated and considered and wrestled with and thought about."

—**Ashon T. Crawley,** Associate Professor of Religious Studies and African American Studies, University of Virginia

"Colin Dayan's lyrical prose is haunting, it oozes through the hot, humid, and putrid air of the deep South calling her back as if to ask her to finish her thought after all these years. This memoir feels like a lucid dream dipped in magic realism. The languid posture of the mother melts into the bull's body distorted with pain, meanwhile the crickets are noisily rubbing their legs in anticipation of sex. A mesmerizing tableau."

—**Bénédicte Boisseron,** Professor of Afroamerican and African Studies, University of Michigan, Ann Arbor

"Colin Dayan's stories of mournful intimacy with animals bring the entanglement of our flesh and bodies to light, a light that seeps through her sweaty, lyrical, Southern memories. Hauntingly beautiful, these musings warn us of our profound precarity."

—**Lori Gruen,** author of *Entangled Empathy*

"In exquisite prose that recounts her mother's passions and demise, the gatherings of humans around husbandry and slaughter, and the dense psychic weight of racial caste systems and anti-black violence, Dayan brings to the fore an enmeshment that tethers her grief and memories to animals that inhabit the south. She writes of how memory flows through the blood and circulates in interspecies relations. I am left with her words: "there is no story about humans that is not also a story about animals.""

—**Nicole R. Fleetwood,** Professor of American Studies and Art History, Rutgers University

"We are mistaken to set ourselves above animals—our pets, our domesticated resources, our wild dangers, our prey—which we only understand in terms of our ability or failure to control or possess them. Dayan's poignant lyrical journal shows that they are conduits to our deepest memories. Seeing history through them, we may learn to yield our claims to dominion and mourn the present that our power has made."

—**Vincent Brown,** author of *The Reaper's Garden: Death and Power in the World of Atlantic Slavery*

Animal Quintet

A southern memoir

COLIN DAYAN

PROLOGUE

—

I thought I was writing a memoir about my past. The more I thought about that past and returned to the South of my childhood, the more I realized that animals, not humans, were what I needed to think about. In all my work, early and late, I have known that reason is a problem, not a privilege, that lives lived close to the soil and in the flesh have much to offer, and not just for anthropologists (or nostalgics), but for anyone who longs to know another kind of politics beyond the wrack and ruin of humankind.

This meditation marks a return to the South and its often raucous racism, a hate so visceral, so non-cognitive, that it can best be known, I have come to think, through the tracks of the non-human: the animals that suffer in the destruction we have wrought against all species, vegetable and mammalian, everywhere.

I have no interest any longer in the mimetic 'I,' in representing myself, so all my journal pages, kept safe and carried around for so long, are now set aside. The past worth writing about can only be apprehended through the non-human, the animals whose eyes, flesh, and sinews lift me up and through the destruction we humans—I need to say it again—have wrought against species, vegetable and mammalian, everywhere.

These are also political stories, evidence of extinctions small and large, cruelty that comes to us as entertainment, racism that rears its head in songs about animals, loved or hunted, killed or kept. The connections are there. This is a natural history, an answer with bare hands to such pro-slavery apologists as Edward Long or Bryan Edwards.

Get down with the fauna. See, feel, and remember, to echo Walter Benjamin, with a twist and reversal: there is no story about humans that is not also a story about animals.

THE OLD
GRAY MARE

—

The chickens came home to roost. I am back in the South. I had my head grabbed by a high-stationed man at a dinner party. Another man, a professor, screamed at me over drinks. I never lived in a place where it takes so much energy not to feel. Not to hear the crickets crackling like banshees outside. Not to look.

There is no real light in Nashville. The sky is rarely blue. In the morning it comes out dull white like bad milk in a glass.

But I did not always see it this way.

When I was young, people were mean to me. Now as the heat rises, back in Nashville, I remember it as horror. Horror, always, on the outside of everything that mattered. The women with translucent white faces, the clubs where people rode to hounds, the parents who could not bear to look at me, the swagger, click of the hand and sway of the hips of my mother's friends—all alien to me.

But still I came back to Nashville, and my discontent with the sodden skies comes fully upon me. It comes in a memory of horses.

As I was leaving the East Coast to return to the South, my child-hood place of horror, I fantasized that I would ride again: a dream of horses, fancy dress, intensely white women and imprudent men. Wrapped up in the gauze of illusion, I thought that once in the South I would become beautiful. I would be what my mother had dreamed for herself, had dreamed into being until decay set in.

Whenever I think about my mother, I think, too, about horses: un-flagging in beauty, ready to die for someone else's desire. Slowly I realized where I was. I had come home.

Nashville's Iroquois Steeplechase began in 1941. It has run contin-uously every May for seventy-eight years except one year during World War II. An old tradition, horses running and jumping for three miles in Percy Warner Park no matter the heat, an all-too-human rite of spring. On a grass track of different elevations, horses try to clear four-foot and six-foot and higher hurdles of artificial brush and timber. The finish line is called "Heartbreak Hill." Most people who come don't watch the horses. They drink, flirt, gossip, and bet on a winner. A choice setting for human do-minion, the race is grueling for the horses that must run rain or shine, but high romance for guests.

The women wear big hats. The men's faces shine from drink. How much do you love horses? Enough to watch them die. To watch their bones break. To watch horses, stricken from too much heat, fold into death.

When my mother began to lose her memory, one song stayed in her mind. She looked at me and sang, as if throwing a curse:

> The old gray mare
> She ain't what she used to be
> Ain't what she used to be
> Ain't what she used to be

Old age had always been the thing she feared. To keep it at bay, she pumped her palm under her chin, slept on her back so wrinkles couldn't set, put the whites of eggs under her eyes. The dreadful inevitability of rot hung like a pall over our house. Everyone, she told me, would end up with loose jowls and cheeks caved in, bags under their eyes and a shuffle in their walk. No one could be young forever. And "no one," she whispered, "loves you when you're old and gray."

As I remember my mother and her broken life, I can't stop thinking about horses. I remember the dazzling War Emblem.

Like the shadow of a bird in flight, War Emblem haunts me. He was fierce. Some say ill tempered. In 2002, I watched this roaring beauty of a horse win the Derby and the Preakness only to miss the Triple Crown because of a sudden drop to his knees when he tripped out of the gate at Belmont. He rose up, tried to run, but could not sustain his speed. He was a horse of big heart and kept going after stumbling, his nose scraping the dirt. He came in eighth. Retired to stud in Japan, he didn't like most of the mares. So he came home to Kentucky.

Four years later at the Preakness, Barbaro fractured his right hind leg in more than twenty places when he prematurely broke from the gate. After six surgeries and laminitis in both front feet, he was finally euthanized. A year later, Eight Belles, a filly, came in second at the Kentucky Derby. Just as she crossed the wire at the finish line, she suffered compound fractures in both ankles. She could not be moved off the track. Instead, euthanized at once, she took her last breath where she fell.

The horses keep dying. The humans keep watching.

Overbred and made beautiful in appearance but weak in the legs, horses are instruments of possession, reflecting the marvelous cruelty of ownership. And so my father chose my mother, his own prized object of beauty. He loved her as long as her dependency was assured.

A plump rather rounded woman of just seventeen, she was chosen by a man some twenty years older. Just a couple of years after marriage, the soft face of a woman beguiled became impenetrable in its beauty. A veneer set in over her luscious skin, hardness took over eyes that were once inviting, her smile frozen for the camera. And the body, sculpted into the image of my father's dream, with hair done up so that it flowed too perfectly, appears brittle in its elaborateness. I think of her now like a hobbled horse.

And that's why I can't get the horses out of my mind, an appeal to freedom that always bit the dust, a possibility of glory that could only be realized in the gaze of others. The South was not kind to my mother. It lured her with a nature that she could never be part of, a community of women that would always be closed. I, too, look at the pale creatures with faces never threatened with sweat. And the lonelier I become, the more I understand the lineaments of discrimination. There are places that I can never be. Out in the green fields, hills and valleys of the "Hillsboro Hounds," foxes are still chased by the most glorious dogs to the sound of "Tally-Ho," and anyone well outfitted and saddled posh enough can look forward to the Hunt Ball at the Belle Meade Country Club and never need be justified.

Something about the Club lured me when I returned to Nashville. I remember a dinner during my first year back. In a wood-paneled room with large paintings of Nashville elites' founding fathers, a black man dressed formally in what I recall as a tuxedo, although it might have just been a black dinner jacket and bowtie, took our orders. It reminded me of a club I knew well in Atlanta. The Standard Town and Country Club, originally on a great deal of greensward with a roiled and challenging golf course and swimming pool. Whether in the locker room or at the bar, a black person, man or woman, was at the ready to serve me. A Jewish club, it was founded in response to the exclusive Piedmont Driving Club and Cherokee Town and Country Club, which allowed only white Christians.

Nashville, the "It City" so popular with *The New York Times*, reminds me of Atlanta in the sixties. To explain why would take me away from horses, hunts, and the triumphant beauty of old money and its manners, the politeness that covers contempt or, worse, disregard. It was in Atlanta that I learned to covet what I was not and could never be. So many blondes with long straight hair, their quiet assumption of place, the easy and alluring confidence of good breeding, a heritage of immaculate inclusion that was never at risk. Not even if you sleep with your best friend's husband or drive too fast, wrecking a stranger's car and killing the person inside it.

Such aplomb and ease are essential to the long history of the South, a tradition described by words like "chivalry," "bravery," "beauty," and "grace." Outside all that, I lived out my life in Atlanta as a child and teenager, watching, and in the quiet of my room, pretending that such a heritage was mine. Such pretense never worked. How could it? I still see my mother coming into my room. She grimaced as she bent over. Then she dragged her feet as if pulling something of great weight. That grinding shuffle terrified me. Not just because of my mother's quick transformation from beauty into beast, but most of all because she reminded me that no matter what we did, how we looked, what we wore, we would always be nothing more than bodies halfway to wrack and ruin.

The only time my mother smiled during her last days of slow but steady dissolution, when she stopped talking or eating, was when she sang the words about that horse.

> The old gray mare
> She kicked on the whiffletree
> Kicked on the whiffletree
> Kicked on the whiffletree

It was eerie to watch her living so fully again only to belt out a song that drew attention to her decline. And she knew as she kicked one leg out in front of her that she was punching out every last day of her life in time with the mare's thrust at the whiffletree.

I stared as she stamped her feet in time with the words. I'm sure she had no idea what the word "whiffletree" meant. I always thought it must be a tree that had been hobbled. In those days I would have said beaten. The tree was beaten. The horse was kicked. It was a world without mercy.

Curiously enough, I never thought about the song's meaning, never questioned its insistent hum in my mind. I never thought about the words I kept repeating, not knowing that "hobble" is not just a limp but also something people do to animals, especially horses. It means to tie or strap together the legs. They are hobbled. They can't move. They can't stray from their fixed place. Why, a friend once asked, are you so compelled by this old gray mare? Now I know: it means to be held by a past that can be captured, all of it, in just a few words. Those words hold some kind of key to what really matters. Transfixed but unable to know exactly why, I am never free of their grip.

She kicked on the whiffletree. Or is it at the whiffletree? I was astonished this spring, when the horses ran again at the Steeplechase, to discover in casual conversation with a neighbor that a whiffletree has nothing to do with trees. Dead trees. Trees chopped down. Death and unseemliness and domination.

Draft horses—the horses that carried the loads for humans—were attached by a harness to a crossbar made of wood called the whiffletree, which was then fastened to the center of whatever was being pulled. Whether they pulled vehicle or plow, cart or sulky, these mammals, with the whiffletree positioned between hock and upper thigh, labored heavily or moved briskly under the load. Either way, it was tough for the horses, at work or in sport.

Both tree and horse suffer for our whims. I was right all along. The tree was beaten. The horse was kicked. Not crucified—that would be granting something momentous to what is commonplace. But everywhere, trees and horses are cut down and flogged. Not much of a matter, it seems, to the minds of humans.

On a hot Nashville day, I decided to return to my mother's song, which meant thinking again about that soft, gently winding track, where horses ran, folks cheered and money was made. The song is a history of America after all, not just the South, not the South of azaleas, rhododendron, and magnolia buds. Here is the full version I am tempted to believe she might have heard back in the 1940s, when she married my father and moved to Atlanta.

The old gray mare
She ain't what she used to be
Ain't what she used to be

Ain't what she used to be
The old gray mare
She ain't what she used to be
Many long years ago

The old gray mare
She kicked on the whiffletree
Kicked on the whiffletree
Kicked on the whiffletree
The old gray mare
She kicked on the whiffletree
Many long years ago

Not a children's song with all the possibilities of changing words and phrases in rowdy innovation, but rather a recitation that closed down hope, a forlornness driven home with the chant, "She ain't what she used to be/Ain't what she used to be." That is the lesson I carried with me: No matter what you do or how you live, the only certainty is that you will always lose the ground from under your feet. The refrain has to do with damage and defect, a leaning always into a state of loss, the mourning that comes with a glance in the mirror.

But I also began to realize that in thinking about my mother I had blocked out some of what matters most about the song. The posture of ruinous pleasure—a delight in stoking the embers of loss—contains a history of pain that has much larger significance than mere pathos. To seize upon the identity and reach of the old gray mare is to recognize the plight of servile creatures, the cruelty of lost causes, and the violence of genial disregard.

Who wrote the song? One guess—no one seems to know for sure—is that Thomas Francis McNulty wrote it during the re-election campaign of the aging Ferdinand Claiborne Latrobe for Democratic mayor of Baltimore in the 1880s. Old mayor Latrobe used to go around in a carriage that was drawn by an old mare. Folks were so entranced by the song and the tumbledown mayor and his horse that he was re-elected not just once but twice more. What manner of mare (or mayor) is this? I find it impossible to believe that this neat story, now the Wikipedia assumption, is the real mystery behind the words. Or maybe I should say that it's not the gray mare I came to know.

I became consumed in a way I could not have imagined, captivated by the early Southern country fiddlers who sang about old mares along with possums and "niggers." It was a constellation of things suggesting decrepitude or disdain, but all covered over by the patina of glory, the spark of fame, the lure of courtliness.

Nostalgia seems to hark back to something displaced or discarded "long, long ago," but more than longing for something past it is actually an emotional connection to something very present. The old gray mare is alive and kicking in the strangest of bodies, animated by our nostalgia. Most Southerners of a certain age found a dream of something in that song. What has been lost? What ideal vanquished? Could "gray" signal not just aging, but something more portentous, something more dire than what I understood as a child? I began to think that the story of the Confederacy might be locked in that song. A battle lost, a cause denied, a region ruined. I began to think of the ruination of all the horses that once ran so beautifully in the big races.

Before he became president, the strapping Andrew Jackson helped set up the Clover Bottom Track at Nashville. Racing was, always, big in the South. Horses mattered to the myth of beauty stored in the sinews of men: their loins astride their mammalian mount. They also bore the pesky contradictions of slavery on their backs. Slaves were used to care for and train horses. Black slaves rode Southern horses. Elevated from the fields, some became remarkable riders. Even after Emancipation and right up to Jim Crow segregation, most of the jockeys were blacks, riding fifteen of the first twenty-eight Kentucky Derby winners. Horseracing and slavery seemed to go hand in hand. By the 1920s and 1930s, like a noose being tightened, hate was strong as the lash, and among its many products were the Georgia-based band Skillet Lickers, famous for songs such as "Run, Nigger, Run" and "Nigger in a Woodpile." Lynching was epidemic. If you were lucky enough to live, a gift of mules with forty acres replaced the brutal aftershocks of slavery.

With the soft shoe of minstrel insult and the meticulous terror of the KKK, history took a turn into a dream of wisteria and lazy laughter. Living in what might seem like dead-end poverty, Gilbert James ("Gid") Tanner, chicken farmer and lead fiddler of the Skillet Lickers, could belt out with gusto unexpected refrains to their country version of the inimitable "Old Gray Mare." The mare kicks at the whiffletree in dilapidation that somehow energizes instead of enfeebling:

> I danced all night
> With a hole in my stocking
> Down in Alabama
>
> I got a great big house
> With nobody living in it
> Down in Alabama
>
> I got nothing
> And nowhere to put it
> Down in Alabama

White lives also still found excitement in the gasp of the starting bell and the lure of courtship set against the breathless run of horses. When the South lost the war, its brutal, sweet and vanishing world was kept alive in their gently curving haunches.

I learned about the high, nearly magical sentience of viscera and flesh as early as elementary school. I am still entranced.

The fragile fiction of high-minded defeat was captured in portrayals of General Robert E. Lee astride his warhorse Traveller, a gray American Saddlebred known for his high spirit, eagerness, and endurance. So imagine with me now.

The loss of the war meant the loss of that old way of life. But this song brought it back. If you listened to it enough, you might feel yourself sitting proud high on this horse that would not quit. If you sat long enough and held loose on those reins, you would fight and never lose again.

I grew up knowing that I was a not-quite-right, too-dark white, but proud nevertheless to be witness to something steadfast if not serene. I along with my classmates—I won't say friends, I had no friends—held on to a drowsy kind of knowledge. We knew the South fell in "The War of Northern Aggression." In the sound of crickets and the smell of magnolia, I became part of a stubborn dream, a dream that rode. I wanted a horse.

I lived for horses. My breath caught when I first put my foot in a stirrup and lifted myself onto that wondrous heap of flesh, digging my foot deep into that tight leather loop.

But now I am driven by the obligation to know why the old gray mare had to grow so old, and how one of the legendary race- and even war-horses, Traveller, has become in my memory the most sorry and forlorn of animals. My mother's lament, in the old days, long ago, is not mine, not exactly the way I see it now. The oppression so manifest across the borders of human and horse sometimes gets concealed under other stories, stories that form a relentless narrative of displacement. It never ends.

In a letter to the artist Markie Williams, General Lee described his courageous horse in exquisite understatement, as he remembered long night marches and days of battle: "I am no artist Markie, and can therefore only say he is a Confederate gray." After the war, Traveller accompanied Lee to Washington College in Lexington, Virginia. There, admirers, mostly students, pulled out the hairs of the horse's tail for souvenirs, giving the horse, in Lee's words, "the appearance of a plucked chicken."

Traveller, like his tail, began to disappear, overtaken in the national imagination by a horse from an earlier generation, the tough and winning mare, Lady Suffolk of Long Island, who has been identified as the real source of the song. The black jockeys who ran the best horses before the Civil War and after, winning the Derby in legendary races, were displaced by white jockeys during Jim Crow and were themselves turned into lawn jockeys, with their bulging eyes and lips with too broad a grin. But in the midst of all these images and stories, the song stubbornly remains, its creator as unknown as ever.

Lady Suffolk. The old gray mare of Saratoga Springs, who raced under saddle or with a two-wheeled sulky, merits an entire chapter of Edward Hotaling's *They're Off! Horse Racing at Saratoga*. But his story suggests nothing about waning strength or loss. Lady Suffolk was what she used to be, and kept winning until her death at the age of twenty-two, carrying her cart, and beloved by all who saw her. A Northern horse, she captivated in the 1840s, at a time when Southerners still traveled North to the track at Saratoga. Edgar Allan Poe came up from Philadelphia in 1842.

The lady gone gray with age, the trotting Lady Suffolk of Northern fame, replaced the gray stallion of the South's greatest general in the imagination of Americans. What does it mean and why should it matter that the lady of the North obscures for all time the warhorse of the Confederacy?

A half century after Lee's gray mare, another gray horse thundered onto the scene of battle, the mare that fought at the front during World War I. "The Old Gray Mare" Newsletter, sent to members of the 109th infantry, nicknamed the "Old Gray Mare Regiment," published in January 2002 a loving farewell—"Best Wishes, Old Gray Mare" —to a sixteen-year-old mare ridden by Colonel Millard D. Brown, as he led his troops across the Italian front in 1917. You can hear this version of the song on the web. Sung by Arthur Collins and Byron Harlan and recorded that same year, the words are punctuated by the sound of guns, the neighs and hooves of horses.

The old gray mare was
Fighting at the front
Fighting at the front
Fighting at the front

The old gray mare was
Fighting at the front
Many long years ago
Many long years ago

Men kill and sing. The horses carry, rear up and die. Songs get written. Everything animal that is not human becomes material for our entertainment or pleasure. Nothing wrong with that, I guess. But in reflecting again on my mother's life, I can't help but think how we so casually take sheer beauty and grind it into the dirt, or more exactly, use it as ballast so that we can float through the carnage we wreak instead of sinking into it.

So perhaps the gray mare is just a token, an excuse for me to wallow in what I thought I wanted to escape. My mother's liveliness and her gorgeous self deteriorated like the gray that began at the roots of her hair. But what is that to me? I can never leave the South. I am held to its rotten romance despite knowing the vileness beneath.

I also realize that the damage done to the bodies of horses often happens against a backdrop of laughter. Southerners like the macabre, and that's why the best jokes—and some of the oldest songs—begin in the least likely of places. Out of the rapid-fire joining of cruelty and pleasure comes the peculiar lilt to a song like "Oh! Susanna," as well as "Run, Nigger, Run." This perfection of white power is not unfeeling. That is its terror. Listen closely to the music and you realize that what really gives the chill is the affection, the near empathy with the lost, the stricken, the harrowed.

These songs are not soothing. And perhaps that is why the high and changing old irrational violence of the South never quite goes away. It remains locked in the senses, this way of life, even for those who claim to abhor its catastrophic racism. I saw Al Jolson in one of his last blackface performances in Darryl Zanuck's *Swanee River*, which first appeared in 1939, though I saw it in the late fifties. I learned that I could never know one moment that would be genuinely free of fear. Something about his eyes lolling, and what I always saw as his white tongue, led me to understand that even gaiety meant nothing but misfortune and trouble.

I grew up in a dazzling social surround, quite unlike the hurt and harm of my home life. In that larger world people lived as if high spirits must always win out. The enigma of lightheartedness kept these folks aloft, above all the evil. They knew how to feed on the remains of what cried out in suffering or died unnaturally, lost to calculated harm. So on the bus up to camp in Asheville, North Carolina, we sang loudly the raucous songs of the South. They were actually laments, but I didn't know that then. "My Old Kentucky Home." "Mammy." "Dixie." "Way down upon the Sewanee River." We never sang "The Old Gray Mare." Only my mother sang that.

I'm back in the South, now, where it's impossible not to think about how the domesticity and chatter and ease are almost always accompanied by something grotesque. The sweetest habit of ladies depends on the shattered life of whatever or whoever is granted neither leisure nor mercy. A few days ago a friend told me about an antique her mother had found, after a long search, an object from some time after the Civil War, though it persisted in homes through the fifties, kept close by all women who darn or sew. It comes in all colors and sizes. It's an antique, a thing to be cherished. Though I never saw one before, I gradually understood that I can't kick myself free of its traces. My whole life has shrunk to this one icon, now faded but once blood red: a velvet pincushion in a horse's hoof.

GORING

BEAUTY

I try to arrange the photos. Black and white, they were developed by my father sometime after his return to the South from a honeymoon in Mexico. I do not know what to call the man in some kind of embroidered costume that looks vaguely Spanish. He is a killer, but a killer with a flourish. He spins round the bull and spears it, looking down so gravely at the stricken animal. No, the spear or sword or lance is already in the shoulder, broken in two, over the raised wreck of flesh. So what is he doing? In one photo he holds a cape. It must be red. Isn't that the story I heard? "Bulls don't like red," my father told me. So one flash of a cape, and the bull "goes mad."

A pile of twenty-four photos lies on my desk. I recognize the same man in thirteen of them. I know him by the waves in his hair. Is he a matador? Or is it the picador? The one who stabs and pierces flesh. My father. Sweet Edmond. Kind Edmond. The bull's legs catch my attention. Holding tight under the shock of a strike, the legs paw the earth, digging up the dust, kicking back in a stretch too graceful for the vile if choreographed assault that means death. The great glory of man, dressed up and ready to harm. The head of the bull turns and dips toward the earth, as one front leg seems to find balance. All I have is the dizzying perception of legs spread and angled, holding on, digging down. The face of the man fades into the black thick pelt of the bull. I search now for expression in the eyes of the animal so assailed by the vain spectacle set to the prance of the killer. All I want is to catch some sense of the bull's feeling, sufficient in attentiveness, the will caught in photo after photo, until the end when the body falls to earth, stilled in the shadow of the man who struts and looks out at his admirers.

When my father and mother married in 1939, they moved from New York to Nashville and then left for Mexico. They arrived in their Buick 8 just a year after Malcolm Lowry's *Under the Volcano* begins and around the year that Lowry left, drunken and misbehaving like Hart Crane and others before him.

I do not know any details. All that remains of the visit are hundreds of photos. There was never any need for words.

No one ever told me stories. It was all drinking and drama and yelling and worry. More than fifty years, over half a century later, I look at the photos, pulled from deep under other albums, moved from out of my mother's closets in Atlanta to my study in Nashville.

Those days were not remembered. They were not part of anything I knew, nor did they make up any kind of beauty that my parents might retrieve about their past, a past when they might have

known either love or passion. I spent my life not knowing the difference between the two. There was no warmth in my house, no sight of a kiss, except once or twice when my father tried to peck at my mother's lips as if he was ashamed, a moment in time preserved for me now only in her grimace. Lust I knew. The long afternoon phone calls when my mother rested on her bed behind a door that was not quite shut. Her legs I could not see. They were under the sheet. I remember a hand moving quickly. Yes, between her legs. Yes, as she laughed and sounded different than usual. Or was that love, as one hand languidly moved up and down, and the other held the phone very close to the ear.

But now before me, there on my desk, I try to get through my father's cracked leather-bound albums. A gift, a glorious preservation of a past otherwise lost forever. These photos from the first months of their marriage lie in wait for me. Once I look at them I might know something beautiful that I did not know before.

My mother's face is always composed, alien. In one photo, bent down, stooping in the dirt and surrounded by parrots, she seems dead, her smile frozen for the camera. A bracelet on her arm and a tan on her flesh, dressed in white and hair pulled back, she looks down at the birds. But she is not really seeing.

Then there is the pose of glamor. Looking out at my father. Maybe she saw this fashion somewhere in some movie of the thirties, the hand drawn up on the hip, a sultry beauty.

Some of these photos are laid out ten to a page, the page is black hard paper; the pictures one upon the other are taped down. To look through them I must lift each one separately, look at one at a time.

My mother never looked at the photos. She had no interest in revisiting the past. I did. Once I moved to Nashville, the past began to fill the emptiness of my life. It came forward when I least expected it. I look again at her photos, lifting them up out of boxes as though they were dirty. It was just the way I felt going through my mother's bedroom dresser drawers at home in Atlanta, fingers into the bras and panties, pulling them up and finding drawings of bodies in poses with a penis in hand or a tongue on the buttocks.

But the bulls are different. The bullfights are on large 8x10 prints. Taunted, prodded, stabbed, the animals know what it is to be killed by humans. They sense that something distinctly upbeat comes along with their suffering. They hear the glee in the shouts from the stands. What, I wonder, along with the bulls, causes such elation? It seems that the more stricken the animal, the louder come the euphoric shouts. I look at the photos. The people are white. Whatever their nationality, their skin is white. Some of the men smile. Others look entranced by the bull's persecution. They all wear suits. And what about the women? I am looking at their faces. Two women are smiling next to each other. Are they getting ready to laugh? Another woman breaks into a wide grin. Some look bored. One smirks. Another turns to her friend. Is she looking away from the dying bull or sharing a joke? None look amazed or troubled.

If I look through these photos long enough, I begin to lose interest in the audience, perhaps because they look as if they might be anywhere in the South and not so far away from me as Mexico. Then, I look back at the bull. There. As I look through each photo, I find something that pulls me into concern, a regard that will not quit. Not something so broad as torment, not the horrific wariness then involuntary capitulation of the bull and its body of flesh moving steadily toward ruin, but instead things that touch my heart more strongly than I could have anticipated: the spin of a tail in a semi-circle, the slight lifting up of a head, then a mouth shut tight or faintly open, the tongue unseen, a head bowed as the legs become straight, poised while preparing to stand precisely in the site of pain. I try to look at the eyes. The black of the bull is so deep that it is difficult to see something as definite as expression. Most of the photos were taken to get the conventional shape of the conflict, the black mass of bull and the costumed curves of man. But in a couple of photos, I can see brightness, an indecipherable touch of light, a bull's-eye view of the dismal panorama of cape flung out, the tormentor's feet rising from the ground, as the dirt flies up into the eyes I had just begun to rely upon as something not marked by death. I feel now that each photo confirms suffering that is effectively without end.

The marriage was doomed. My father went to the bullfights. The man rides the horse, a carnival picador dressed as if for a state fair in Georgia, spearing the bull. The bull is real. The bull is too gorgeous to be killed. More beautiful than my mother, or at least alive to the touch in a way she could never be. As I remember my mother and her broken life, I can't stop thinking about the bulls, the many bulls isolated from their kind, released into spectacle, performing their agony, the light in their eyes slowly turning into dark.

Dust, photos, pile upon pile. It hurts me to look at them. So I took all the photos, hundreds of them in albums, cases, loose, or whatever—and put them back in the garage. But I kept the bulls dying in effigy on my desk.

This is a story about how bulls die, the blood, the curve of horns, and the lift of a head in response to the matador's formal low passes. The bull's head is raised high as the body collapses. But the legs are strong in their denial, the poise still fierce even as the legs stand apart. Some writers suggest a shared physical delight between human and bull. I do not see that reciprocity in these photos. It is an invention by humans and for humans. In *On Bullfighting*, A.L. Kennedy describes the "curious, intense dance between two species ... as blood wells out of the bull's wounds." But what kind of sharing could be had in such an encounter, and why do writers so often recall it as rare evidence of the reciprocity between species? The progression of the *corrida* from mutual alertness to the matador's deliberate stalking and the bull's growing exhaustion signals a peculiarly human cruelty. Terrible and majestic, yes, but also absurd: self-importance masked by the stiff brio that comes across as play. "It is up to the bullfighter to make the bull play and to enforce the rules," Hemingway reminds his readers in *Death in the Afternoon*. Then he adds, in a sleight of hand that gives his writing assurance at the very moment when it falters in glaring abstraction: "The bull has no desire to play, only to kill." I look at the photo, with the bull's back torn by the *pica*. Not a spear, exactly, and not a sword either, but a pick, a narrow wooden shaft with a steel point. Broken, the stick splinters in two.

I have no choice now but to look through the series of photos that portray the matador—at least two different men in more than one fight, one with a ponytail and the other with a short coif, both in embroidered jackets—and the bull in the final passes of the cape, the still small step of the bull, a final surge,

a momentary charge that is disrupted by the body that now seems heavy as lead, in places already caving in, soon to collapse, wounded, head lowered in a gentle arc, flanks heaving, tendons and muscles strained, legs bent with the shadow of his scrotum sack and the end of the tail spinning so fast that the hair become feathers catches hold of my attention. Many times I look away. My mind drifts somewhere else, wondering why I no longer care about a honeymoon that left my mother cold, my father clueless. But not for long, since I am drawn again, brought to focus by the bull's legs. They tell me all I need to know about phenomenal grace and something more than beauty, for how can feet fixed in dirt, then raised up in the air at the strike, muscled with life then holding on in death, a head swerved gently, perhaps nodding in recognition of hurt, be anything but compelling, more absorbing than the flourish of the man with the cape? I place all my hope in the fleshy pads of the underside of the bull's hooves, in the head hanging weighty and too low, in the tail that never ceases to move soundlessly through the air, and in one back leg pushed out straight either to move the bull forward or to keep the body still as the head turns massively into the cape. This cape is doubled over a wooden stick or rod. It is called the *muleta*. When the *muleta* appears, everyone knows this marks the third and final stage of the bullfight, when the bull is weary or *aplomado*: in Hemingway's words, "he has been made heavy, he is like lead; he has usually lost his wind, and while his strength is still intact, his speed is gone." Now the sword will be used.

Death by cape and by sword: In one photo I have before me, a sword and *muleta* held out in one hand, and in the next, the sword in the right hand, the *muleta* in the other.

I have tried to put them in order, these photos that stay on my desk. Thousands of negatives remain in the brown boxes in the garage. Perhaps they contain images my father chose not to develop in his darkroom, so late at night, when my mother had already turned her back on him.

During the time I spent looking through the pile of photos, arranging them in some order that might make sense, a growing sense of unease took hold of me. I stopped writing. Now when I go back to the desk I face pieces of a performance that no longer hold together, that cannot be made whole. I read again descriptions of the bullfight, as it should be or was, the ritual in three parts with only one correct way of killing the bull, of rousing the crowds, of exhibiting the splendor and exact formality of the matador, of death.

Again I take the photos and spread them out, all of them. Here is the picador in this single photo of a man on horseback, all a'jingle with his short jacket and tight breeches, like any other bull-fighter except for the crazy white hat that sits on his head. And then there is the horse. Is he blindfolded? Horses die, and no one seems to mind. Even Hemingway admits the horror of such a death, entrails falling away from the wound, though he can't resist identifying disemboweling as "one of those strange and burlesque accidents" so integral to the experience of the bullfight.

There are no *banderilleros* or flagmen in sight, not in any of these photos. So I sit here at my desk and see quite clearly the bull pelt made jagged, the flash of metal against the dazzling sun. Into that part of the neck, atop the hump where muscles ripple between the shoulders, comes the goad: as the bull tosses his head, these men plant barbed sticks that pierce the skin. Splendidly colored flags, paper strips, even ribbons are attached to these stick-blades, making a mockery of torment. Under this flutter of color and after many tiny stabs, the muscled hump between the neck crest—the place between the neck and the top of the shoulder—is weakened, the muscles relaxed, the head lowered, so that the sword can go in for the kill. Now the bull collapses. Wearily, he sinks to the ground, resting, it seems, on one horn.

The sound the sound the sound, I repeat to myself, what is the noise heard when the bull knows he is being murdered, when, deadly tired and pierced to the bone with picks, darts, and the ultimate lance thrust, he cries out in the arena to the cheers of a crowd? No one, as far as I know, has written about the noise a bull makes. No one cares about the death rattles and groans, the bellowing that shakes up the performance with a strength that will not suffer humiliation.

The bull is dead in the sand, so huge and lost that he reminds me of a harpooned whale that has been washed to shore.

"Toro, toro," I hear the words in my mind. That nearly imperceptible memory comes to me now. I recall how we used to play bullfighter in my backyard late in the afternoon in the heat of another Atlanta summer. The game consisted of someone flashing a red scarf, or maybe a sheet of any color, in my face as I ran toward it.

That was all: the lift of a cloth and my mad dash through it and beyond into some place where I lay along the dark earth in dead silence. There I remained, hidden, my mouth open. I did not want to be the bull anymore.

WHITE
LEGHORNS

—

"**The** best is yet to come, and babe, won't it be fine?" Frank Sinatra's voice, that pulsing timbre and liquid phrasing came out of the den as my mother drank Scotch with friends and Thomas the yardman slaughtered my hens out back. He got the rooster last. Blood on the carpet, the lush green grass, as the white leghorns ran without their heads. I looked on through the screen on the porch. They were my chickens. I had raised them from their days as cute little yellow symbols of Easter cheer. They became real. I loved them. They grew, they pecked; they played and ate.

I tried to make ghosts out of what remained of their flesh but was left with nothing. Axed at my father's behest, their bodies kept moving after everything else died. No more scratching the soil, no more hunting for bugs or worms. They ended up in plastic bags in the freezer without their heads. No feet either. I'm not sure whether Thomas took the heads and feet home to cook. Lucille, the woman who raised me, swore he did.

Something like fate hung around my house. No way around it, that's what my mother told me. "Once something bad happens, it will happen again." My rabbits ate their babies. I buried my turtles alive, thinking they had died when maybe they were just in hibernation. My mother's canary drowned in a glass of water. My hamster got stuck and died behind the stove. But the chickens were slaughtered. That was different. Not fate but cruelty. Not accident but expediency.

Why not eat the white-feathered animals with deep brown eyes? What else were they good for? The rooster crowed. Neighbors complained. I begged my parents to spare the hens. My father said they were useless since they never laid eggs. My mother said they smelled up the yard. Lucille, as always, had the last word. She told us, "They ain't nothing like a fresh cooked chicken." She didn't like animals, thought they were more of a nuisance than even her husbands, four of them, all dead already.

Everything around my house was so casual. Everything seemed to happen to the tune of Sinatra's singing. So now I listen every chance I get to his station on the car radio. I can't get enough of his chic and casual disregard. Even in a lament for a woman he loved now gone, there's buoyancy, a boozy kind of pleasure, the lingering scent of sex.

So here is the scene. Chickens run amok, their bloody necks like nubs of flesh across the grass. Thomas stands by the fence with the axe. Their heads lie around the yard like fallen apples.

WHITE LEGHORNS.

FROM BIRDS SENT OVER SPECIALLY FOR PORTRAITURE BY Mr SIMPSON.

TREASURER OF THE NEW YORK STATE POULTRY SOCIETY

My mother with a drink in hand stands on the porch. Then she grabs me by one arm and pulls me inside. Her friends laugh. I hear Sinatra. "You ain't seen nothin' yet/The best is yet to come and babe, won't it be fine?" Nothing was good ever. Even the best meant the worst. I heard his promise that sounds like a sweet threat, "I'm gonna teach you to fly," and thought about my chickens when they took to the air, never for long and never very high. But I loved to watch them rise up pumping their wings and take a short flight to the fence or the top of a perch. Even with their heads off, I thought I saw a couple when running lift off the ground. I heard another Sinatra song. I couldn't stop it sounding in my head. "Come fly with me! Let's fly! Let's fly away!"

Have you ever looked into the eyes of a chicken? Chickens see color differently than humans. Besides seeing blue, red, green, they also have an added wavelength: ultraviolet light. When Thomas raised his arm to strike at their heads, perhaps they caught the glare of the silver-flashing light axe against the sky. In one of the hen's last moments, she might have seen like a star the sheen of metal, and like the sunset a spurt of blood. I think now that her head might have bobbed more than usual at the moment the axe hit, tilting her head much further sideways than normal before it fell clean off her body. I always heard that when a rapacious bird flew by chickens bent their heads with their left eye up to the sky. That's because the right eye is near-sighted, good for looking for food in the dirt, while the left eye is far-sighted, ready to search for predators. That afternoon when the women drank and Frank sang about that "sunshine day," my chickens were looking at the axe come down like a bird of prey, and they could do nothing about it but run. And run they did, without their heads.

I can't help now thinking about the scene of butchery against the lure of lovemaking. The chase, the chop, the violence, and the blood became the background to the supple innuendo of Frank's voice inviting his listeners, on that day my mother and her friends, to get wooed, kissed, and fucked.

> You think you've flown before, but baby
> You ain't left the ground
> Wait till you're locked in my embrace
> Wait till I draw you near
> Wait till you see that sunshine place
> Ain't nothing like it here

Rapt up into "that sunshine place," somewhere out of this world, the ladies of leisure drank their whiskey and lay back against the sofa, feeling the flush in their cheeks while I stood outside listening to the sounds, knowing my chickens' panic, sensing their eyes staring up at the arm with the axe. A strange spectacle: I watched their bright red wattles, flaps of skin that dangled below their chins, hanging down so loosely, it occurs to me now, like labia swollen with blood, red and deep, sensitized by the immense profanity of that hot, languid afternoon, the afternoon I lost what I loved.

Years later, Thomas told me the story of their death. Out in the back of my house, there were five white hens, he told me. I thought there were five or six. One of them, the very beautiful hen, kept running back and forth, "not wanting to give up her breath," Thomas said. "She was a tricky girl, hiding in the bushes and trying to warn her chicks. She was clucking and crouching when I found her, ruffling them feathers hard as she could." A few years after that conversation was the last time I saw Thomas, just a few months before he died. We sat together in the house in Atlanta. He had just made an hour walk from the bus stop all the way to our house, and again he remembered the chicken blood in the rain. "White feathers," he said, "made for clean picking." Then he reminded me: "You cried all day long. You caught hell," Thomas said, "for looking out the wrong side of your eye."

In the late afternoons when Lucille and I argued over who had control of the channels, a pale woman appeared on the tube like a sibyl, as if announcing my defeat in the contest about what got watched as she advised viewers to take St. Joseph's Aspirin. "Can 'headache' describe this quivering pain ... when every movement of your head brings on an agonizing spasm?" *Quick Draw McGraw*, *Popeye*, and *The Mickey Mouse Club* lost out to Lucille's favorites: *Maverick*, *Cheyenne*, and *Rawhide*. The only cartoon Lucille wanted to watch was *Foghorn Leghorn*. Maybe she thought I'd get over my leghorns' deaths if I could start laughing about the mischievous, fast-talking rooster with a Southern accent. Or maybe she just wanted me to feel sad and never forget that, whenever someone wanted to, they could take what I loved away from me or kill it just like that, as quick as "it took an egg to fry," she used to say.

Lucille joked with me about her four dead husbands. She loved to tell me how they died. She laughed and clapped her hands at the really good part: when the scythe split open Ben's foot as he cut Florida cane or when Joe Moses got caught in a cotton mill and lost everything from the torso down. "What you gonna do when death comes creepin' in your room?" she asked me one Saturday afternoon. I told her I would ask God to forgive me and bless his name. She said that I'd do better to say nothing and just get ready for the ride to the other side. But when I asked her about my white chickens in the freezer, wondering whether it was a sin to eat what suffered, she told me: "Legguns should never have been white anyway. They used to be brown, but once they got to America they turned color. So they got what they asked for."

The South. That is how I knew it then. The place where things got cut up, chopped and sliced, where body parts appeared in windows at night, if you turned around on the wrong side of the bed or fell asleep on your back. When I lay down and turned off the light, I saw my chickens bobbing their heads, tilting them toward me. They appeared with their beaks torn off. Down the hall, I heard my mother laughing. She laughed on the day when I caught her out front in the den with Bernard, her best friend's husband. No shirt, just a bra, and whatever she wore from the waist down, I don't remember. When I ran in the kitchen and told Lucille, she said something about "dead skin" and "dust," warned me to keep my mouth shut and pushed me outside on the porch.

The dust of love, the end to hope, that is what my mother taught me. Back I go into her voice, into the song she repeated again and again, only a few lines of it, when I least expected her to break into song.

> Our Love, I feel it everywhere
> Through the nighttime
> It is a message of the breeze
> I can hear it
> In every whisper of the trees
> And so you're always near to me
> Wherever you may be
> I see your face in the stars above

Tommy Dorsey in 1939, a foxtrot with Jack Leonard singing. That is what she heard when she was young, the year she met my father, before the snap and sizzle of Sinatra and her louche carrying on with fat, old men. I heard the song again on the radio a few days ago in Nashville. I recognized it. "And so you're always near to me." My mother came rushing back. The sound carries me home, and then I'm back to the time when I danced to Romeo and Juliet, *en pointe* with my flat feet, knowing that Tchaikovsky's overture came before Tommy Dorsey's band and my mother's disappointment.

Lucille understood what I wasn't supposed to see. She shoved me out back. Out there—I remember, I see it still—she scratched in the dirt with her feet, just like a chicken. Whenever my mother was home, there was no telling what might happen. Her women friends might lie around drinking Scotch and telling dirty jokes or she might be in some mess on the couch with Sinatra in the background. But of the things I saw Lucille do, the thing she seemed to like doing most was fry chicken. And that's what I still see in the kitchen whenever I think about sex.

I never knew what had happened to the wattles and combs of the chickens, though I knew Lucille saved the gizzards and neck for herself. For us, she cleaned those chickens down to the innards. Once the entrails were dragged out, she put her hand inside and took out anything red or loose. I could hear laughter deep in the house. But I concentrated on what was left of my chicken; perhaps this one in the sink was the one that panicked, staring at me one last time before being caught. Even though Lucille cared, she couldn't take seriously my sadness. It was just like a white, she said: "Just like a white to feel bad about the wrong things."

Whenever Lucille and I took our walks in the early evening, she told me stories, usually having to do with the onset of summer. It was a time of abandon always held in check, that familiar tug at the gut. "Crickets rub their legs before having sex," she whispered. "That's the sound we hear. It's no song. It's them aching for love." Then, she'd stop still on the sidewalk, look at me, and begin to imitate Louis Armstrong. Why she did this a block or two into our walk, I still don't know. But it was a song about chickens, as well as a curse, and it came out with a grunt and a smile. No last sigh, no final words could haunt me like this anthem of summer.

> Now I'll be glad when you die
> You rascal you, uh-huh, I'll be glad
> Oh I'll be tickled to death
> When you leave this earth
> It's true, oh yeah
> When you're lying down six feet deep
> No more fried chicken will you eat

She knew that white folks had to be watched. "You'd think they be walking straight, but before you know it, they turn around and kill you just like your father killed your hens." When I said that Thomas axed them, she looked at me, and spat: "And what he going to do? That black fool. Stand up and say 'no, they your daughter's hens?'" She laughed in my face.

The crickets got louder.

I was caught between my mother's sins and Lucille's words. She spoke to everything in the house meant to be kept dark and secret, but uttered it low, reminding me that all desire came to grief. Life was inconsolable. Nothing was direct, but a hint of harm to come, an omen of evil just waiting to fall across my path, as surely as my foot would slip. Chickens clucking in terror on the bloodstained dirt, human eyes rolling in rapture or mockery, the jewels my mother wore, the soil on my dresses, the lovemaking that surged to and fro in my mind for a long time, all of this came into view not just then but years later. Whenever I heard a love song, I saw blood. No man could kiss me without my feeling the brown soil in my throat, the hole dug to stop my hens from running away, taking flight, lost in the dirt forever.

The air felt different after my chickens were killed. Pigeons squatted on the roof beyond my bedroom window, and the sky was gray. Animals never lived long in my house after that. Too much cruelty resided for too long in that place not to make a shroud that hung over us all. My parents were cruel to each other. And to me. My father stopped listening to his favorite music: Mohammed El-Bakker and his Oriental Ensemble and Dvořák's

New World Symphony. Sinatra's *Songs for Swingin' Lovers!* lay on the floor, unheard, along with Nancy Wilson's *Yesterday's Love Songs, Today's Blues*.

Lucille died. Thomas alone remained constant, telling the stories about chickens running for their lives and my crying self. He also laughed a lot, especially when he repeated: "I'd never tell a mule good morning." Years later, I understood that this was his response to the dubious gift to freed slaves of "forty acres and a mule."

I left home and never returned to Atlanta, except for funerals. Lucille died, then my father and mother. Thomas died last of all. At night I sometimes see Lucille on her couch turned toward the wall to avoid what she called "night terrors." My mother still looks at me out of her exquisite whiteness, though that appearance, too, was just a feint, an imitation of life that was never hers, though she seemed to move through the house in a flurry of light and silken speed, a ghost before she was dead. My father hated all animals, so I don't have much to say about him here. I remember how he kicked my puppy across the room and tried to knock me across the head. I've reckoned over the years with his superlative mind. He lived by ordering others around, by ignoring whatever he could not control, by acquiescing in prejudice as long as it came masked by common sense.

Did you ever make a wish on a chicken's breastbone by cracking it in two? No, that's not it exactly, and I want to get it right. With the wishbone, like the rabbit foot, humans took a part of a dead animal and turned it into a talisman, a proof of good luck or promise that you might just get what you need. So we always dug the forked bone, between the chicken neck and breast, out of the meat and left it on the windowsill to dry. Then, we stood facing each other, Lucille and I. We pulled it apart, each taking one end of the divided bone. We both made wishes silently to ourselves. But I knew that the only wish to come true was that made by the person who ended up with the long end of the wishbone. I can't remember anything except the sound of the snap. Anything after that didn't matter.

"To burn always with this hard gemlike flame, to maintain this ecstasy is success in life." Walter Pater's words stayed with me for a long time. But how to carry on in this flaming world of experience when I smell dead flesh, when I hear the fierce sharp cackles of my hens or hear the lone rooster crow, going long into the night on the day they were slaughtered. I'll never know how many chicks were hidden under their mothers' wings, and anyway it would be too horrible to remember. The hens stretched their necks, looking this way and that, with the eyes I so often looked into like pools of ebon water. Now one last time, they turned, not quite sure where or if to run. "Stop squawking like a damn chicken, or I'll whip you with this belt," my father shouted at me.

Now that I am in Tennessee I know why I want chickens, back-yard hens on this land. The South of hard drinking and slow talking nights where lightning bugs flicker and crickets sing never left me. Not even though I tried to kill the deep, real sight of what I kept looking for without knowing it: the eyes of chickens. And oh they were smart and wily. I know that now. I understood why the hens lived long and fought hard to keep on living, why children mattered and mothers cared. It makes me giddy, as I happen to glide over a past that I thought long gone, lost to view in this world of commerce and ashes, where even the smallest bird in flight is a wonder. I am giddy as the white leghorns return.

Possum
Hunting

—

One

night late I let my dog Stella, a spirited Am Staff, out to pee. A few minutes later, I heard a deep, throaty groan, that last gasp of an animal dying. I thought she had been hurt, ran out in my robe, and got her in the house. When I went back out, I saw eyes looking at me like stars. I took a photo. It was a possum.

But as soon as I saw it, it flopped on its side, teeth bared, eyes staring fixedly into the dark. I thought for a moment that it had died. But it was just playing dead, "playing possum."

At night the men took their rifles and went out to hunt possum. One cool October, I went out with Lucille, to meet her nephew and his friends. My parents were away, so I could spend the night over at her house on Ponce de Leon Avenue with her and her sisters Nellie and May. But first we were going to do something different. She wanted me to see what it was like to be out in the woods with dogs and men, to follow them and look up into trees or scour along the ground, not hunting but just following the men who went out after these little animals. I remember nothing but how Lucille held my hand, how bright were the flares of light—not flashlights but wood sticks burning—and the sound of crickets.

Lucille used to tell me that her father was only happy when he talked about treeing possums with his "first-class" possum dog, which jumped up, barked, and whined like the dickens. She laughed. Took a step forward, hand on her hip, and with a sashay sang, imitating Fats Domino: "He got his thrill on Blueberry Hill." She invented new words for what she liked to call (when night fell) "the time of the possum." Possums were the only animals she didn't hate.

> The moon stood still
> On Blueberry Hill
> When that big rascal
> Shone his eyes on me
>
> The barks of dogs
> Led me to that tree
> Where possums smelled bad as hogs
> But playing dead can't fool me

Hot and wet and summer with crickets and mosquitoes, that was the best time to go out and look for possums. We never found one. Never even saw its eyes. But might as well have done. Listening to Lucille, I could see that possum right in front of us and hear a hiss. I saw tiny babies in its pouch, and I didn't want it to be killed.

Walking with Lucille on summer nights, I went back with her into a past when, she said, "The only thing a nigger could have was his dog to corner possum." Nothing could compare to the glory of possum soon to be carved, its meat baked "brown as my skin" with potatoes and greens. "The little pink nose and those claws on five-fingered feet," she sang, "nothing is better to eat than a possum so tough but so sweet." When I used to visit Lucille and her sisters, I learned what counted in life. Possums were good animals. They ate up all the ticks, even slugs and snakes. "Well," Lucille told me, "they'll eat just about anything. They ain't particular, not picky like you."

When the subject is possums, questions of good and evil, blame and fault come to life in sharp relief. Years later, I found a possum song in a book called *Slave Narratives After Slavery*. William Wells Brown, the fugitive slave, abolitionist, performer, best-selling writer and author of *Clotel, or the President's Daughter*, wrote a memoir called *My Southern Home; or, The South and Its People*. It was published in 1880, nearly forty-six years after he escaped from slavery. Describing how whites catch "negroes" with dogs, bloodhounds, lots of whipping, and worse, he writes with nostalgia for the South but also with hauteur about African Americans who find themselves slaves: "There was considerable truth in the oft-repeated saying that the slave 'was happy,'" though it's "a low kind of happiness." He adds: "History shows that of all races, the African was best adapted to be the 'hewers of wood, and drawers of water,' … the negro is better adapted to follow than to lead."

Then he pauses and gives readers a sense of the beauty of the night when work was done and slaves sang in tribute to the pleasures of possums they hunted and trapped. They knew all the while that the same dogs trained to hunt slaves could tree a possum:

> De possum meat am good to eat
> Carve him to de heart
> You'll always find him good and sweet
> Carve him to de heart
> My dog did bark, and I went to see
> Carve him to de heart
> And dar was a possum up dat tree
> Carve him to de heart

The possum hunt joins hard-nosed cruelty with warm familiarity. It sure was fun to see these nasty creatures, set dogs on them, and shoot them dead.

White people didn't always eat the possums they caught, though even now I hear people say that it's a delicacy, better than any other kind of white meat. And if they had babies in their pouch—"as tiny as honeybees," one man told me—even better. I wanted to know more about these creatures so mocked by the white men I feared growing up. They called them "meat flaps," as well as other words that scorn women's private parts.

But African Americans saw possums differently. They did not scorn them but reckoned them to be marvels of adaptability, wily and brave, like that "possum up the gum stump" with his "jaw black and dirty." That didn't mean they didn't hunt them. But they went after them with a certain respect. Also, their beloved dogs were with them, what they knew as their own best things. So I understood what Lucille's final husband—the last of five, and also not long for this world—meant when he explained:

> You got to know what it was like. Night comes, suddenly dogs bark, and we see them there eyes. You know, possums got eyes that glow in the dark. They shine like candles burning in a pitch-black room. And then they stop right in their tracks, dead as can be. But they're alive. Just playing possum, sliding themselves sideways close to the dirt. So you just go up and surprise them, real quiet and calm. Real trouble comes when dogs tree a possum. Then you got to shake the tree. But you can't always be sure that will bring it down. And the dogs going wild, and we getting fed up. But you got to hand it to them: possums know what they're doing.

Lucille used to read me stories about "Brer Possum" from Joel Chandler Harris's *Stories from Uncle Remus*. Before the possum meets the snake in "Brer Possum and the Snake," we learn: "Brer Possum is one of the nicest animals you'll ever want to meet." He'd give "you the fur off his back." These stories, told by a kindly ex-slave, were part of the African American folk tradition. One of Zora Neale Hurston's earliest stories, "Possum or Pig?"—published in *The Forum* in 1926—takes up that old story of "High John de Conquer," the legendary folk hero and slave who outwits his master when he passes off a cooked pig (stolen) from the farm as a possum.

Shaved legs. Suntan oil. My mother's best friends embrace. I've moved out to the porch, right in the sun. Laughter went along with heat. Zenobia and CG Becker were the women I loved to watch. But Molly, my mother's best friend, had a thing for possums. "Gone possum hunting," she said. "They got pussy and the men are going after it." Pussy and possum, there's something to it. And she knew it. Tall, too stout to be statuesque, she wore a lot of makeup. She looked like she was in drag.

Molly walked into the den, looked at me, smiled, and said with her head tilted to one side, "Goin' possum huntin'." Her words stayed with me. As a child I wondered why she looked at me the way she did, and why she spent so much time saying "possum," which she drew out into a sound like "paws some," her mouth turned into a tight oval, pink and wet. Later I knew what she meant as she ventriloquized men that she would have known only from afar. The innuendo was her dirty joke, suggesting that's how "white crackers" or "white trash" act when they get together. Men talking about a hunt, whether for possum or pussy, it didn't matter much. Or that's what Molly would have thought of their ways of loving you. Animals all: the white men and their women; the white men and their possums. But in her eyes they were nothing more than material for a performance of the lascivious, and it found safe and perpetual life in this projection of everything she never had to know except as the butt of a joke.

Cruelty comes in many forms. Chasing possums by the light of a cold white moon with rifles and guns and dogs is a game of terror. "Playing possum" was something everybody could do, no matter where they came from. And we all did it. We made ourselves dead, not like any old corpse, but just like a possum, feet splayed and eyes glaring. There's something in that: a way of lying down, a manner of thinking about swamps and piney woods and dissolving into dirt. But nobody I ever knew could imitate the sound a possum made under threat: a sizzling kind of wheeze, so guttural that you imagined someone's throat had just been slit. Screaming through the blood in their throat.

Possums become receptacles for the fiercest outpouring of human emotion. The hunt brings to life a drama of conflicts and affiliations with long histories. There's the noise of the chase: dogs yelping, horns blowing, possums wheezing and grunting. The other night I listened to Gid Tanner and His Skillet Lickers sing "A Possum Hunt on Stump House Mountain." I can't find the lyrics. People tell me they're racist, which I'm sure they are. I can't rightly hear what they're saying although I listened to them singing more than once. Such a good time, fiddling wild and quick, and the banjo strumming low. "Down in the holler running a coon ... blowing the horn." But the possum can't be caught. All the men are imitating dogs. It's the wildest thing to hear, this rowdy rendition of a chase, a chase that could be, as the song would have it, after any old "coon"— you know, raccoon or black person—or just after a possum. A whole history of the South is in the possum hunt.

I asked an old neighbor what he thought about such a song. He never did hunt possum, he told me. "But I know the words of that song," he explained, "and they have a strict meaning. If you got nigger blood and try to pass for white, that's what they're singing about." As I listened to him, I began to understand a history of shape-shifting. Better, one of color changing, that told the story of a racist South. Not like race hatred in the North, where you just stay away and keep separate and refuse to acknowledge, but instead a rollicking immersion in what you most fear. So when Tanner sings out amid the barking and hollering, "Ain't no possum, polecat," what he means is that what you just chased and caught is not what you thought, not what it appeared to be. Something is wrong. No possum but a skunk, and, damn, it stinks.

The hate must be known. And what kind of knowing is that? It is a knowing that must be shared and passed down to those who did not live in the time of the possum. And it comes out with laughter. How about those possums? I want to write "them possum," and must stop myself. How much else am I censoring? What is it about possums out there in the night that returns me so fully into the smells and sounds of my childhood that I stop, knowing that I keep going around and around on certain words? Words cover the sight of bright eyes in the dark and the sound of fear in the night. So let's begin to know why possums matter more to me than skunks, raccoons, or any other critter of the dark.

When my dog Stella was just six months old, I began to scream out, "Tree it, tree it," as we walked down the street. Out of what memory did the words and the vehemence come? Even now, when she is nearly crippled with a debilitating disease of the spine, she jumps upside of that tree. Something is in her, something of the past, a past that she never knew, that is in her blood just as those words are in mine. We share the visceral memory. We return to some kind of passion, a special kind of pleasure, and I see again what the hunt is all about.

Leave it to Americans to make nastiness out of an animal hallowed in Native American and Mesopotamian mythology. Possums are not what might be expected in a backyard animal. Mysterious, even magical, they are also mistreated and abhorred. I call them "possums," but I could have said "opossums," a word I never heard growing up. If you look the word up in Merriam-Webster's Collegiate Dictionary (as well as the Oxford English Dictionary), you'll find that opossum comes from two Virginia Algonquian words that mean "white" (op) and "dog" (passom). White dog. Both pest and spirit, lowdown and exalted, these creatures cross boundaries between the familiar and strange, the real and mythical. They recall the sacrificial and sacred White Dog of the Iroquois, "spotless" and "faithful," or something lost to evil enchantment, locked in white skin.

The only marsupial in North America, with hairless ears and off-white prehensile tails, they boast five-fingered front feet and four-fingered rear feet with an opposable thumb. The feet are shocking to see, so pink and the nails clear and white, just like human fingers. Could they once have been humans? Possessed by an evil spirit, did they turn themselves inside out and, while taking on possum skin and fur and shape, retain consciousness and will?

When it comes to reproduction, the possums' anatomy makes them vulnerable. Waywardness and ambiguity herald eradication. How to speak plainly about the male's penis, bifurcated like a two-pronged fork, but, more pressing, how to grasp the female genitalia? Early colonists thought mating took place through the female's nostrils. She then sneezed her babies into the pouch, sometimes called the "purse." The truth is that like all marsupials, females have triple vaginas and two uteruses. Children's books about possums abound, but these curious details are nowhere mentioned.

Drop that possum. Shake the tree and watch it drop. Here's a "Possum Song" sung by Everett Griggs, a white man in Clinton, Arkansas, as late as 1975.

> Now, if you shoot that possum
> Just sugar 'im good an' sweet

Put 'im in a little fryin' pan
Sweet taters around his feet
Just put in lots of gravy
Right next to the crust
An' what'a ya gonna do little children
I'll eat till I bust, bust
Bust, bye-bye t' that possum
O, bile the possum down
Bye-bye t' possum
When the possum hits the ground
Bye-bye t' possum
O, bile the possum down
O we'll have a good dinner
When the possum hits the ground

You can "bile [boil] the possum down" in the pot on your stove. Or you can drop it from the tree when you shake it hard to the sound of your dogs barking below. Or, in what I still think of as an unimaginably unseemly ritual, you can celebrate the New Year by dropping a possum like the "ball drop" at midnight in Times Square.

In Tallapoosa, Georgia, the city once known as "Possum Snout," the ritual "Possum Drop" is announced each January—"New Year's: The Possum Drop, Tallapoosa, Ga." Music. Fireworks. Family fun. Entertainment. Just two years ago, the website announced that a crowd of over 10,000 people celebrated. At the end of the announcement, with photos and telephone numbers to call if you want to be a sponsor, there's a "NOTICE": "We Do Not Use A Live Possum— It Is Stuffed!" The effigy possum named Spencer in a wire ball with Christmas lights is suspended around 11:30 at the top of the American Hometown Realty Building and "slowly lowered" at midnight.

But up until five years ago in Brasstown, North Carolina, at Clay's Corner gas station, a live possum fell to earth. In those days, the owner Clay Logan explained, the possum, trapped by hunters and fattened up until the big night, was lowered, not dropped: "If we said, 'Come to the lowering of the opossum,' well, nobody would enjoy that," Logan said. For all those who think putting a live possum in a Plexiglas cage, subjected to the sound of fireworks, yelling, and shotgun fire and then being dropped from a great height is cruel, Clay assured his interviewer Bill Geist for *CBS Sunday Morning* in 2011 on "The New Year's Dropping of the Opossum": "As a matter of fact, there are probably opossums up around my house with little signs saying, 'Use me next year!'"

When PETA sued Brasstown, the "Possum Capital of the World," for animal cruelty, the organizers began using a dead possum. How the animal died, whether legally hunted or already dead from "natural causes"—in most cases, roadkill—did not matter to PETA. As long as the possum did not suffer, the show could go on. The North Carolina legislature passed a law to issue possum permits by the state wildlife commission, and the event resumed a year later. There's no bag limit on how many possums are killed during hunting season. But just a year ago, a living possum again became part of the festivities. The website for Clay's Corner assures us: "We just want to let you know that we do ABSOLUTELY NOTHING to harm the 'possum. We celebrate in honor of this marsupial!"

Depending on where you sit in this country of ours, the ritual is either tender or brutal. Asked whether the farewell to the possum as he releases it is "a stirring emotional moment," Logan answered: "Well, you know, we say goodbye. We don't kiss. But we say goodbye." What a hoot to see a possum dropped from on high—whether booty, roadkill, hunted, or living—and men dressed like a cross between women, possums, and men. Logan said, in an article in *The New York Times*, it's a joke on redneck culture, "which I'm entitled to do, because I'm a redneck." Entitlement. You make fun of cracker culture, but you also have a right to transgress race and gender—as long as you're a white man in the South. "Next year I'd love to get me an albino," he laughed. "They're rare … But imagine that. An albino possum drop."

Lucille always told me, late at night when we went out back, that I didn't have much to fear. I was too light-skinned to "make them bitter and mean." But in following the track of the possum, I see the bond that joins whites and blacks together. It's an old tie and a terrible yoke. Whether hunting or skinning or cooking up possum, whites and blacks share a history. But they share it contradictorily, feel it differently.

On a possum hunt in the night with guns and dogs, ghosts still haunt the earth. I hear their death rattles. They are possums and persons liable to destruction and killed with impunity. What happens to these animals in the South can tell us a lot that we need to know about a certain kind of easy stigma. Pursuit and eradication are forms of knowledge, ways humans hone their fury. Possum eyes, possum flesh and sinews, suffer through the destruction we have wrought against all species, vegetable and mammalian, everywhere.

People complain that possums are still around, but I never see them anymore. I long to see one in the night. To me they're not a nuisance, but a test of memory. If I saw one of these animals out back amid trees and undergrowth, I'd still myself, go dead in my limbs, look into its eyes, and remember that it used to speak, a spirit totem on uncharted land. I'd give it a chance to live again in the light of the moon.

Boll weevil blues

"You only cross the sea of the dead one time," my mother told me. "You only cross the shore of the dead one time," she said a few days later. That time we were sitting in her bedroom. She seldom managed to leave her bed, with the piled-up lace pillows, silk sheets, and the telephone ringing, as she liked to boast, "off the hook," which meant without letup. Her readiness to laugh and joke was granted to her friends, not to me. I bored her. Only when she took the opportunity to share with me her grim maxims did she shake herself out of lethargy. With sweet malice, she spoke with an enthusiasm that I never knew, except as a threat. Now recollecting those moments scares me, even as I crave the sensation.

Her feelings for me were never hidden. Even though she's dead, I know she enjoys reminding me how much she matters. Her words and songs can still crowd out whatever I'm doing. Quite unexpectedly, I hear her sing "All the Way," as if she still wants to bring into light hidden things of darkness. A love that must be hidden, although as she knew it never did lie still but grew more intensely the more it was off limits. So she sang: "When some-body loves you/It's no good unless she loves you, all the way."

Years later, I feel the thrill in hearing it sung by Sinatra. Her desire remains tight in me, just as it did then. She meant it to. And deep, deeper than the deepest sea, "that's how deep it goes if it's real."

Deep like the knife that went through her stomach. Years later, in my one-room apartment in New York, beginning the Ph.D. that she scorned, I fantasized about taking a knife, stabbing myself, and bleeding to death. I lived in thoughts that could not see the light of day, but now I know that the secret, this tinkering with mortification, had become the language we shared. "For if ye live after the flesh, ye shall die: but if ye through the Spirit do mortify the deeds of the body, ye shall live." The words of St. Paul in Romans get mixed up with the beauty of my mother's flesh, the unearthly look in her eyes, and her demand before she died that I give up everything I had worked for and come to her in her home wherever it was. She wanted me.

Lost or gained, love came along with injury and distress. My love for my mother has brought her close but not without loss of appetite and sleepless nights. "When are you coming home, Joanie?" she would ask. I'm coming home in the only way you understand: by turning toward you like a plant leaning into the sun, losing what was mine only to know you again: in your refusal of food ("eating like a bird," your friends used to say), in your burns while cooking, or your fluke accidents.

On a visit to the dump where I tossed the week's garbage, I was hobbled with a bad crack to the ribs, as I bent over against the seat of the car and reached for the bags. Lying here now, unable to move without pain, I hear another one of your favorite songs: "All of me." Standing by the couch where I lie propped up on pillows, I hear the words, "Why not take all of me?" As I look over to the stairs, you are there with one hand reaching out and a voice that seems to reside inside me, rising and falling on my every breath. But we are not home. Deep in the fog that has settled around the house and listening to the rains that won't quit, I sense how restless you've become. I become filled with your favorite song of surrender. More than your complaints about my looks, once you left the South to join me here, you became as battered as I am.

So whatever belongs to me, I give to you piecemeal but strong, just as you gave me lips that never kissed and discarded arms that never held me:

> Take my lips, I want to lose them
> Take my arms, I'll never use them

Such romantic longing seemed in retrospect to be somewhat extravagant in its style of self-abnegation. Full-out narcissism came to life through this performance of love that found its peak in giving away body parts. Such surrender was willful and gruesome, if you stopped to think about it. But I never did. Feeling was all: an instant of abandon that mattered more than a lifetime of care or devotion.

Not for Lucille, the wistful declaration of love through relinquishing arms, feet, or lips. No such fascination with Peg Leg Bates. That was just the "icing on the cake of cruelty," as she used to say. Instead, I now come to realize that Lucille's stoop and the stomp of her walk before me some afternoons, with the stork-like stand on one foot leaving the other free to hit the floor toes first, might just have been in homage to Peg Leg Joe, the peg-leg sailor who led slaves to their freedom.

> De riva's bank am a very good road
> De dead trees show de way
> Lef' foot, peg foot goin' on
> Folle de drinkin' gou'd

I never heard her sing the whole song, but she shouted to me during our long nights alone in the house, as she came stooped and crouched around the corner outside my bedroom door, "lef' foot, peg foot goin' on." Tap, tap, tap went her left foot as she imitated the sound of a wooden leg, moving closer and closer to me as I hid under the sheets, just waiting, just breathing in the darkness until that moment when she shouted real close to me, "Boo." I can still feel the warmth of her skin so moist near me, as I let her lips rest close on my neck.

Her South became my own. That is why I long to be there no matter where I am. She made magic out of loss. That wonderland waited for me in her songs, but most of all in her stories. They were love stories that could also freeze me with fear, as she remembered a past that might have broken her. "No I ain't broke," she told me and let me know where she found glory, what gave her delight. All we had to do was go outside, even at night, and let our bare feet touch the earth, our ears keen to the sound of crickets and what she called "the earth shimmers." One night I trembled in the cold as she talked and turned the backyard into a field, the azalea blossoms into cotton bolls. Picking cotton. One husband cutting his foot in two with a scythe, the other husband leaving his torso behind in a cotton gin. In the diminished dust of a vainglorious land, Lucille summoned the ghosts of her husbands, and we dreamed together into that place that refuted my mother's glitter and sentiment. There was no room for my mother's louche escapism in this moonlight of affliction.

More than the praying mantis, or the grasshopper rubbing its legs together, or crickets or June bugs shedding their shells, the boll weevil casts its intransigent shadow over everything else. You might say that cotton remained the center of Lucille's life. I never thought about her family, who must have been share-croppers after slavery, who lived close to the "cotton fields back home," and suffered the ravages of the boll weevil assault on King Cotton in the 1920s and 1930s. She adored these beetles, which seemed to exist solely by their miracles of presumption. "Ain't nothing like the boll weevil for bullheadedness." And she sang out words that brought the bug before my eyes. "You'd better treat me right. I'll eat up all of your cotton, sleep in your kitchen tonight." There he walked, as Lucille liked to repeat, "with his ugly self."

In 1962, Brook Benton's "The Boll Weevil Song" reached number two on the top hits chart. But Lucille thought he was too tame for the scourge of the boll weevil. She told me how angry the white people's radio stations made her. "Simpering and prissy," she used to say. I don't know where she got the words that she sang to me. I didn't know enough to ask. "That little black bug," she said,

> had nowhere to go, but that never stopped it from lookin' for a home. And it ain't so mean as they say, but so ugly that folks just found all kinds of ways to try and kill it, but mostly failed. And just when it looked to be

no more boweevils, Lord, there they'd be. These long-nosed bugs never stopped lookin' to find a place to call their own.

But because they had that homeless feeling, they could persist through all the bad things done to them. I learned about the evil humans did, their brute treatment of anything they didn't like, but most of all, I understood that if you could be more like an animal, or in this case, insect—anything non-human—the closer you were to goodness, to the things that mattered, and especially, to love. She taught me that there is no story about humans that is not also a story about animals. On those late afternoons, especially, as we walked outside, I learned what it means to know with the body, to know so fully with the flesh that it is nothing other than mind. Only now, so late in my life, do I understand why socializing always made me uncomfortable, why I looked for any other kind of creature that might be around, so that I could find eyes to look in, some kind of flesh that I might feel I could touch.

The dogs were barking. Together in the heavy night we waited for the buzz of mosquitoes. We heard sounds made on the grillwork of windows that tinkled like crystal. Lucille summoned the white hand, its pure emergence into the porch where we sat. "Jesus," I said. And she responded, "Oh, sweet father Jesus." When she laughed, I looked up into her eyes, then closed my own so that I could wish that these good times, the good dreams could go on. It was there in the hot buzzing summer that I best knew myself. Sometimes the heat went, as Lucille like to say, "into my blood" and made my head heavy. She figured that it was time for us to go in, held out a hand so that I could put mine in hers, and I was covered over, folded up in her skin, safe in her shade, as we turned our back on the moon.

No possum,
no sop,
no taters

———

In a dead zone ghosts cannot live. They need the life that festers, the things that swarm. Whatever decays becomes fodder for their persistence. Now that I am out of Tennessee and on Martha's Vineyard, I note their refusal to be wisps of air, some kind of steam, wet in the night or voices on the wind. They always come in bodies. They need the sensations felt upon contact with objects of matter, the mere feel of leaves underfoot, the pressure of whatever remains: a clod of dirt, a torn scarf, or dried twig. But most of all, they go into the things they loved. And there they make the past palpable. Without the blatant or the wanton, they last uncertainly and not for long. I am certain that their force depends on the warmth of animals: the deer that crowd before the hunters descend upon them; the possums that jump into garbage cans; coyotes, even skunks that bristle in the night. But here there is nothing, only wild turkeys visiting at dawn and dusk. Every inch on this island has been tamed in one way or another.

Lucille, the woman who raised me and haunts me still, will not walk on these fields of brown and yellow ochre. No dogs are barking. There are no bugs. Alone in the night, I listen for her, but all I hear in the long silence are the words, "Hot voodoo black as mud/Hot voodoo, in my blood," and I know that she's speaking to me, like a booming from the past, telling me about hate with a laugh, prompting me to know again how to deal with the dull and tipping tongues of whites. It's no magic. Whites like to sing about or deride their imagined Africa that pulses with the forbidden. Lucille called me out, often in tired self-mockery, "You know you're too brown to be white, but you can't shed what they done to you." It's evil when they gut your substance and replace it with sex, the lure of sin that comes with the mere mention of voodoo. Now here I am in dull winter baffled by a sense that I'm being turned to stone. Without the teeming scent that hovers even in the cold as I walk the streets of Nashville, I become indifferent to the sky and long for Lucille. But she does not come. Even my dog sleeps too much and cares not a whit for the random turkey that feeds on the dirt.

"*Be* careful what you wish for." Or as Lucille used to warn "Buzzards feed on the blood of dreams." I drove to the North as if my life depended on it. My dog Stella, her beds, piles of suitcases filled with wool scarves and sweaters, everything that waited with me for the escape from the moist heat and leaden sky of Nashville, was like ballast for my flight from what I thought I despised.

When I arrived on the island, I was perplexed to find two dead gray mice, bloated in the toilet bowl of one of the bathrooms. In the old oak tree outside, the turkeys loomed ominous as crows. But they would soon stop resting in the grim-barked leafless trees. An old oak covered in fungus, as if tired from fighting the canker of fungi that crept from its roots to its crown, defends its position as forlorn messenger of something as yet unknown.

In the terrible monotony in which no ease is ever found, I sometimes see a few small birds that look like sparrows. Dark gray, they remind me of dead mice. "Dead as a doornail," I hear Lucille mutter. This terrain has been made safe for the old and the wealthy. They have come here to do yoga, eat well, and live long.

Stella stays in one chair. Besides the seeming absence of anything visceral in this space of artifice, I'm certain she also misses the kindness of

strangers. In Nashville, a UPS man laughs and says, "What a puppy! Such a handsome dog," but here in Chilmark she is greeted at the door with what I'm sure she senses as disdain: "Keep that door closed. I don't want that dog getting out." So we live here, missing all manner of sinews and flesh, the sounds of possums and raccoons in the night.

We're sitting together on a day that's far too warm for winter, with a faint chill in the air. A time when life should burgeon. Yes, that's the word, I tell myself, that's when all things flourish and bud anew in the light. But instead, one single fly stays in the house, trees grow mold on their branches, mice hide in walls, and wild turkeys scatter their droppings everywhere. The turkeys haunt the trees like a few luckless mounds of feathers.

When I took Stella to the vet in West Tisbury, a quaint spot on Yellow Brick Road, three women accompanied me to my car in a phalanx. An Am Staff is wonderful around humans but aggressive toward dogs. We all went up the stairs to the reception area together. I slid on the damp wood, landing on my back and shoulder; the vet asked whether I wanted to make a liability claim. Holding my dog still tightly grasped by the leash, I looked up and said no. Once Stella was on the examination table, the doctor told me in a mellow voice to be careful. Stella would be safe nowhere given her breed. He asked whether I had a muzzle for her. I didn't, so they offered me the largest one they had. It was too small. After measuring her head, the vet wrote out on a piece of paper: 10 ½- 11" circumference cage muzzle.

We left with heartworm medication, an anti-tick and flea dose pack, and a shampoo of aloe and oatmeal. Stella has been worse since the visit. She of course became worried when I again got lost in the attempt to get home. The island has three main roads: North Road, Middle Road, and South Road. I kept ending up on North Road no matter how often I went up Tea Lane Road or down Tabor House Lane—the crossroads from North to South or vice versa. With Stravinsky's Firebird Suite playing on the radio, I went back and forth, disoriented. Did some catastrophe await me in the tranquility of these roads? I am in the land of dead rocks, I thought this time round.

Then I realized that I had arrived in the landscape of a poem by Wallace Stevens. "It is an artificial world," he writes in "Extracts from Addresses to the Academy of Fine Ideas." And that's swell because this is a world not only of artifice but also of retired academics. Now whenever I set out to go anywhere, my pulse quickens and my stomach turns. Stella looks over at me wide-eyed. I tell her not to worry, even though I feel that I'm on haunted ground. Not like in the South where the ghosts hover at the end of a hall, in a corner, or croon to you as trains pass by. Here the spook is inside you, rattling the mind and gnawing at whatever had been known or all-too-familiar, in the safekeeping of well-heeled assumptions and privilege.

We are lost. Not just on any road but inside the house that stands alone—I almost said "aghast"—stranded on the waste of fields and woods, desolate of life. Not even winds blow. In what I fear is a dead zone, I've come to look forward to the rain that makes the only sound in the night. But even that is nothing more than the shudder of unwanted things.

There are many forms of death.

A lone turkey is outside dying. Her flock has left her behind. Feet under her belly, she draws herself tight into a mound on the soil and grass, but not for long.

Nothing can thrive if it comes here, into this seared terrain with the dome of gray hovering always above the dry rocks and leafless trees. Not me or my dog or this turkey I had come to know, the "lady" I called her, who braved snow and winds to remain near this house, or so I thought. I too have not been well since coming here, a sudden spike in blood pressure that prohibits my departure, although weeks ago I wanted nothing more than to get into my car and drive back home. Stella sleeps most of the time now, except for a morning walk away from these fields around the house, since she will not walk here. She, too, is fading.

But I was wrong about ghosts. They are here. Not Lucille's kind of ghosts, the orphans crying in the night or the ladies in white scraping at windows, but things malicious that have no shape or magic or memory. Far away from my mother's spirit, hovering still I reckon in Nashville, I am afraid. And I mourn for the turkey that still huddles, dying, looking less and less like a bird as she leans into earth, becoming nothing more than a mound of packed soil.

Two days ago, I noticed a small wooden chair, a child's school chair, and a tiny stepladder inside the porch, both set neatly in front of the sliding glass door. I had never seen them before.

It was then I knew I had to leave.

I had heard Stella barking for no reason at various times in the day. I realized that she did not want to go into the master bedroom where we slept.

Then I saw the photos in the hallway of the old schoolhouse: "The Old Chilmark Schoolhouse." That is where I am. But I hadn't given it much thought until I saw the chair and the ladder on the porch. At the other end of the house is the beating heart of this past. It contains the bath-

room and master bedroom. Though the house has been extended with the addition of a living room, kitchen, and three other bedrooms down another long hallway, it is the old part with the low ceilings that holds the spirits. The front door is now closed off; and though visible from the front of the house, it has hidden one of the two hall closets in the vestibule outside the master bedroom where I try to sleep, which happens also to be the site of the old schoolroom. There sat the children on little chairs just like the one that appeared out of nowhere on the porch.

I should have known that the house was inhabited when the old cape appeared in the laundry room a month ago. All kinds of things had been happening, but I didn't pay attention to them: Stella's apparent discomfort and barking, the sounds in the night, or a constant low frequency buzzing in the air.

Then I discovered in the laundry/storage room a cape with rusted buttons—much like what Melville's Israel Potter would have worn ("the dress of an English sailor"). It appeared out of the blue, lying on my bags. Then I draped it on the vacuum cleaner. When I looked closely, I could see a couple of tawny-chestnut hairs. The coat announced that they were going to make themselves known. "We are coming. We are coming back."

That's when Stella started to become uneasy, when she would suddenly bark, eyes staring out upon nothing. That was also when I suddenly had immensely high blood pressure. It has never been normal since then, not even with medication.

Now that I think back to my arrival, I recall how Stella did not want to enter the bedroom, where for the first two weeks I could not sleep at all. My face became sallow and wan. I aged about twenty years. I didn't know what to do or where to go. The other rooms down the hall in the new part of the house were too cold. But I knew that I was in some kind of danger, as if something was eating away at my life. I awaken every night now, at 12:30 and then at 3:00 in the morning. Winter has come.

Now I know why there is nothing living outside. No deer. No birds. No skunk. No possum. There is only that one dying turkey that I can't bear to see. The large flocks have disappeared, abandoning her. And the howling winds, and the little children who weep in the night so deeply that I can't hear them, even though I know they are there.